Blockchain-Powered AI

The Convergence of Two Disruptive Technologies

Table of Contents

Chapter 1. Introduction

In this special report, we delve into the intriguing intersection of two of the most disruptive technologies reshaping our contemporary world: Blockchain and Artificial Intelligence. Our pragmatic exploration addresses how these two technological powerhouses collide, shedding light on how Blockchain enhances AI's capacities and accommodates its applications, ultimately catalyzing a paradigm shift across various industries. Although technically complex, the essence of this report is presented in an easily digestible, down-to-earth manner, ensuring readers comprehend the potential of this transformative convergence. Whether you're a seasoned tech-enthusiast, an ambitious entrepreneur, or simply intrigued by the future's digital prospects, this report is your compass to navigate the fascinating and, at times, overwhelming landscape of Blockchain-powered AI. Join us on this journey of discovery, unraveling the immense potentials embedded in this techno-duo that promises to redefine tomorrow's digital frontier.

Chapter 2. Unwrapping the Concepts: A Primer on Blockchain and AI

Blockchain and artificial intelligence (AI) are ground-breaking technologies that continue to stun the world with their relentless, innovative strides. To fully appreciate the potential of these techno-giants, particularly as they draw each other into a breath-taking alliance, we first need to grasp their individual essence.

2.1. Blockchain: The Trust Machine

If you've heard of cryptocurrencies, notably Bitcoin, you've already been introduced, albeit cursoriously, to one of Blockchain's applications. At its core, Blockchain is a decentralized digital ledger. Unlike traditional databases stored on a single server, Blockchain data is dispersed across a network of computers, referred to as nodes. Decentralization removes the vulnerability associated with data being stored in a single location, consequently fortifying security.

Each block in a blockchain consists of a list of transactions, which are invincible to adulteration or deletion once added. This immunity imbues the blockchain with a high trust quotient, designating it as a 'trust machine.' Blockchain's decentralized, immutable nature fosters transparency, frictionless transactions, and trust among parties even in the absence of any central governing authority.

Though initially conceptualized to secure financial transactions, the real power of blockchain transcends beyond, enabling 'smart contracts' and the creation of decentralized applications (DApps). This breakthrough technology embraces myriad sectors like healthcare, supply chain, finance, and others, effectuating a paradigmatic shift.

2.2. Artificial Intelligence: Driving Intelligent Automation

AI is the science of creating intelligent machines and softwares, typically exhibiting some facets of human intelligence like learning, reasoning, problem-solving, perception, and language understanding. Machine learning (ML), a subset of AI, allows computers to learn from data without explicit programming, adaptively improving their performance.

Moreover, deep learning, a further subset of ML, utilizes artificial neural networks akin to a human brain's structure. These networks can learn from unstructured data, fostering groundbreaking advancements in voice recognition, image and pattern recognition, sentiment analysis, and natural language processing.

AI's prowess extends to in-depth data analysis, enabling predictive analytics, and fostering decision-making, thereby underpinning myriad applications from autonomous vehicles to personalized recommendation engines. In essence, AI becomes a backbone for automation, revolutionizing industries while orchestrating an era of unprecedented progress and efficiency.

2.3. The Nexus between Blockchain and AI

There's an undeniable synergy between Blockchain and AI, mainly through blockchain's ability to augment AI's capacities while AI ramps up blockchain's efficiency. Blockchain bestows AI with trust, transparency and explainability whilst AI brings efficiency, scalability and automation to blockchain networks. With this symbiotic alliance, sectors like finance, healthcare, supply chain, and many more can leverage immense value, mitigating existing limitations and exploiting growth opportunities hitherto unattainable.

Firstly, AI and Blockchain both handle data, albeit in different ways: while Blockchain manages data transaction and storage, AI processes and learns from the data. The decentralized and immutable nature of blockchain ensures data authenticity and security, crucial for AI systems.

Secondly, the 'smart contract' capability of blockchain can automate AI model governance. As AI models evolve with new data, smart contracts can automatically manage the version control and parameter tuning, reducing the need for human interventions.

Thirdly, AI can counteract blockchain's high energy consumption drawback. By adopting AI's capacity to learn and optimize, blockchain procedures like mining and transaction verification could be streamlined to consume less energy, enhancing sustainability.

In conclusion, while we've seen these disruptive forces make impressive strides separately, their confluence can unravel transformative possibilities. Blockchain's transparency and trust meets AI's intelligence and automation, setting the bedrock for an untamed fusion, the ripple effects of which have started seeping into different industries, fueling astonishing developments that herald a blockchain-powered AI future.

This chapter introduces blockchain and AI, focusing on their individual capabilities, followed by how their integration can revolutionize myriad industries. As we proceed, we'll delve into more complex aspects of both technologies, peeling back layers to expose their immense potential. The following chapters will explore concrete instances of this alliance, revealing how blockchain can underpin AI applications and how AI can enhance blockchain procedures, propelling us towards an exciting new frontier in digital technology.

Chapter 3. The Road to Convergence: Tracing the Blockchain and AI Evolution

Over the past few decades, we've observed striking technological advances, which initially arose independently on their separate paths yet gradually began to intersect: the encrypted, decentralized system of Blockchain and the cognitive, data-driven capabilities of Artificial Intelligence (AI).

The emergence and development of these two technologies have been separate yet somewhat parallel processes, taking shape alongside each other, each with their distinct narrative, before starting to intertwine. This co-evolution has largely mirrored the growing interconnectedness and complexity of our digital world.

3.1. The Genesis of Blockchain

Let's first turn our attention to Blockchain, a technology that was birthed out of the 2008 financial crisis. The foundational idea is attributed to the anonymous entity, Satoshi Nakamoto, who proposed a decentralized, transparent system to eliminate intermediaries in financial transactions. The initial implementation of this transformative technology was Bitcoin, the world's first cryptocurrency.

Blockchain technology is essentially a distributed ledger that reliably records transactions across many computers, ensuring that every bit of data can be traced, tracked, and kept secure. This unique characteristic of Blockchain enables it to act as an immutable record of truth, resistant to fraud, and trusted globally.

From the inception of Bitcoin, Blockchain has gradually been embraced across various sectors due to its potential to considerably alter the way data is managed and transactions are conducted. Today, it has transcended its original financial context, being applied to healthcare, supply chain management, energy, and beyond, thereby evolving into a widely applicable system for secure data management and exchange.

3.2. The Emergence of Artificial Intelligence

Concurrently, on a seemingly separate path, AI began to take shape, edging away from the realms of science fiction and into tangible, practical technology. At its most basic, AI refers to computer systems designed to mimic human intelligence and behavioral patterns.

Alan Turing, often considered the father of AI, posed the profound question in his 1950 paper - "Can machines think?" which ignited the nascent field of AI. Over time, researchers and scientists have developed various forms of AI like Narrow AI, General AI, and Superintelligent AI, each with increasing levels of intelligence and capabilities.

AI's development has traversed numerous waves, often stimulated by advances in machine learning (ML), a subset of AI where computer algorithms improve automatically through experience. Over the years, AI has seeped into various areas of our lives, including healthcare, transportation, and entertainment.

3.3. The Overlap Begins: Blockchain Meets AI

As each technology matured, the inherent benefits of integrating Blockchain's decentralized security with AI's cognitive capabilities started gaining recognition. The two powerful technologies, each disruptive on their own, began overlapping in certain unique areas.

Firstly, AI's necessity for vast amounts of data to build models can potentially be fulfilled by Blockchain's capacity for data management and exchange. Here, Blockchain can enact as the trusted mediator, allowing safe, verifiable transactions of data, something AI requires for accurate machine learning.

On the other side, Blockchain's biggest challenge, transparency in complex operations, can be overcome by AI. The algorithms can analyze and interpret complex Blockchain data, providing crucial insights into the operations taking place.

Thus, the convergence of these technologies promises to overcome the existing limitations each faces singularly. They together offer untapped potential that could reshape the industries fundamentally, ushering a new era of innovation and change.

3.4. The Road Ahead: A Converged Future

The convergence of Blockchain and AI is by no means a completed journey, but the promising outset suggests a future where their combined capabilities are intertwined across various industries. Consider healthcare, where Blockchain could potentially secure patient data, making it accessible only to authenticated actors, while AI could use this data to make accurate diagnoses and treatment recommendations.

The road to convergence is paved with immense potential, but at the same time, it's filled with challenges. Ensuring that this convergence is harnessed robustly, securely, and ethically is crucial. Despite these challenges, the intersection of Blockchain and AI presents an exciting frontier brimming with opportunities.

As we further venture into this exciting new digital age, the combined strengths of Blockchain and AI have the potential to reinforce and transform the way we manage, control, and share information. The dynamic duo promises to catalyze various economic and social changes, thereby shaping a future that's secure, intelligent, and profoundly revolutionary, setting the stage for a new technological paradigm.

Chapter 4. Marrying Blockchain and AI: The Synergy Explained

Blockchain, originally devised for digital currency such as Bitcoin, has now found a more profound significance. AI, on the other hand, is a frontier technology driving the fourth industrial revolution. Blending these two concepts together, we expand our understanding of the intertwined roles they play and the promising future they forge.

4.1. The Basics of Blockchain

A blockchain is best imagined as a distributed ledger collecting data across numerous computers, called nodes, such that each node has an identical copy of the ledger. To understand its potential, you must recognize that blockchain operates on principles of transparency, robustness, and decentralized authority.

Unlike traditional methods, transactions are recorded and timestamped within 'blocks' of data, with each block linked to the preceding one, hence forming a chain. These blocks are decentralized, making it near-impossible for manipulation by any single entity. As such, the information once entered cannot be altered retroactively, awarding the system an unmatched level of trust and security.

4.2. Artificial Intelligence Explained

Artificial Intelligence, or AI, refers to computer systems capable of performing tasks that generally require human intelligence. These can be as rudimentary as recognizing speech, or as complex as decision-making capabilities in evolved fields like autonomous vehicles or robotics.

AI works by combining large amounts of data with fast, iterative processing and smart algorithms. This allows the system to learn automatically from pattern or feature recognition, thus becoming more precise and effective at tasks as they are continually performed.

4.3. Blockchain and AI: An Interplay of Potentials

When considering Blockchain and AI side by side, we observe that Blockchain's core trait, namely its secure and unalterable nature, is a plus for AI. As the decentralized AI models demand data with authenticity, the blockchain system can deliver exactly what AI needs - not just data integrity, but also data security and privacy.

Regarding data handling, AI's real power comes to the fore in its data analysis capacity and decision-making capability. This is accentuated further by blockchain's transparency and traceability, making the results more accountable and audit-proof.

4.4. Advantages of Blockchain and AI Integration

Salient advantages of the Blockchain-AI union bear fruit in multiple fields:

- Health: With blockchain, health records can be decentralized and shared securely among authorized users. AI, in turn, can provide personalized treatment plans by analyzing these records.

- Banking: Blockchain can prevent fraudulent transactions, while

AI identifies anomalies and suspicious activities. Together they ensure a safer banking environment.

- Supply Chain: Blockchain's traceability helps verify goods and reduce counterfeit items, and AI automatizes checking and sorting of items, thus increasing efficiency.

4.5. Future Development

This combination of AI and Blockchain appears well-poised to rewrite our digital landscape. It not only boosts security and privacy but also increases transparency and efficiency.

As AI becomes more prevalent, there ought to be regulations in place to ensure ethical use. Blockchain could provide that by recording each AI decision and its basis on an unalterable ledger. Simultaneously, as we aim for data protection and ownership, Blockchain may decentralize data, and AI could ensure data is used effectively.

4.6. Conclusion

The partnership of AI and Blockchain offers a future, where automation and decentralization coexist and enhance each other. Unquestionably, marrying Blockchain and AI opens gates to an array of possibilities ranging from more secure transactions and immutable records to more robust and accountable AI decisions, marking a considerable step in our digital evolution.

Nevertheless, their integration is not without its challenges, including issues related to governance, legalities, and technical complexity. While these obstacles are substantial, they are not insurmountable; dedicated research and collaborative efforts from all sectors are required to truly exploit and optimally utilize the potential of this synergy.

Chapter 5. Pivoting Accountability: Blockchain's Answer to AI's Transparency Dilemma

AI, with its computational efficiency and data-crunching prowess, has been considered a transformative technology. However, its rampant growth has also cultivated concerns about transparency and accountability. The opaque nature of AI processes, often described as the black-box dilemma, has left users clueless about how AI systems make important decisions. Consequently, this has heightened susceptibility to bias, desirability, and legitimacy concerns. On the other hand, Blockchain, praised for its unparalleled transparency and traceability, surfaces as a promising solution to this predicament.

5.1. Blockchain and AI: A Conceptual Overview

Blockchain, a decentralized technology, records transactions across multiple computers to ensure data security and transparency. These transactions are time-stamped and immutable, creating an unfalsifiable history of events. The emphasis on decentralization, enabling everyone on the network to track and validate transactions, is what underpins blockchain's promise of transparency and trust.

At the other end of the spectrum, AI involves machines and software exhibiting behaviors associated with human intelligence, such as learning, problem-solving, planning, and understanding language. It heavily relies on algorithms and data to make decisions. However, the exact mechanisms through which these decisions are made are largely hidden from public scrutiny, giving birth to the black-box predicament.

5.2. Understanding the AI Black Box Dilemma

The black-box model of AI is a term for AI systems whose inputs and operations are not discernible clearly. Problematically, the opacity of the black box can lead to unintentional biases. These biases may manifest as racial, gender, or socioeconomic prejudices that can have profound impacts on individuals and society at large. Without clear visibility into AI logic and decision-making, it is hard to pinpoint where these biases originate, let alone eradicate them.

Further, this lack of transparency in the black-box model limits the prospect of meaningful human oversight or intervention. Critical decisions made by AI may affect aspects such as healthcare diagnostics or financial lending without an understanding of the processes backing them.

The transparency conundrum of AI fuels mistrust, resistance, and skepticism among users and regulators alike, thus amplifying the call for accountability in AI systems.

5.3. The Intersection of Blockchain and AI

Blockchain can be a game changer in addressing the transparency dilemmas of AI. It introduces a degree of interpretability and explainability not usually part of AI systems. By applying principles of transparency, security, and decentralization to AI, blockchain can enhance AI's accountability.

Blockchain can maintain an indelible trace of each data point processed by an algorithm, allowing users to track how the AI reached a particular decision. This transparent, tamper-proof record of AI processes can foster credibility and trust among users by demystifying the black-box operations.

Further, blockchain's decentralized nature prevents the monopolization of AI technology and its related data. Driving control from centralized entities to a network of users fosters an environment conducive to data integrity and accessibility.

5.4. Harnessing Blockchain for AI Accountability

Here, we delve into specific ways in which blockchain can resolve the AI black-box conundrum.

* **Immutable Auditing**: Blockchain can store records of each AI decision, creating a tamper-proof history. This ledger serves as evidence of AI processes, enabling comprehensive audits that enhance transparency.

* **Secure and Decentralized Data Marketplaces**: Data is the lifeblood of AI. Blockchain technology permits secure, decentralized data marketplaces where data providers and buyers can transact transparently, reducing the potential for data manipulation or misuse.

* **Transparency in Decision-Making**: Blockchain can store each step of the AI decision-making process, enabling users to understand the AI's path to a particular decision. This transparency quells concerns about bias and discrimination in AI systems.

* **Strengthened Data Privacy**: Blockchain's cryptography safeguards data privacy while sharing data for AI processes, establishing data transparency without compromising

confidentiality.

5.5. Future Direction: Regulatory Needs and Technological Advancements

The marriage of blockchain and AI undoubtedly presents a promising way forward for transparent, accountable AI systems. The utilization of blockchain technology to improve AI processes' transparency is a significant step in the right direction.

However, technical challenges such as scalability, efficiency, and the complexity of implementing blockchain in AI systems need resolution. Furthermore, the creation of legal frameworks at a global level to regulate this integration is an urgent necessity. Rules regarding data ownership, privacy, and accountability are needed to cultivate trust and acceptance among users.

The development of public understandings about the potentials and limitations of this convergent technology is also essential. Public-awareness campaigns, educational programs, and stakeholder engagement could ensue a shift in public perception, further driving the adoption of blockchain-based AI.

Ultimately, the convergence of AI's power and blockchain's transparency champions a new ethos in the digital landscape, paving the way for responsible, transparent, and accountable AI. By fearlessly embracing these technological breakthroughs, we can contribute to a digital future defined by integrity, inclusivity, and empowerment. This compelling, symbiotic relationship between blockchain and AI promises not only a change in the way we interact with technology but also a reshuffling of societal norms towards a more responsible, trustful digital future.

Chapter 6. Data Privacy and Security: Amplifying Protection through Blockchain-Powered AI

As we venture deeper into the digital era, the question of data privacy and security necessitates an increasingly vital role. In this context, the convergence of Blockchain and Artificial Intelligence (AI) emerges as a powerful tool to address these challenges at hand.

6.1. The Magnitude of Data Privacy and Security

The story of data in the 21st century is often illustrated as a double-edged sword. On the one hand, data is the fuel powering our digital civilization, spearheading breakthroughs in nearly every corner. Conversely, it poses tremendous challenges concerning privacy and security. With endless instances of data breaches and cyber exploitation, the haunting fear of data misuse is an ever-present reality for both individuals and corporations.

Even raising the issue of data privacy creates a paradox because adherence to privacy norms sometimes undermines the very essence of AI. AI's core prerequisite is vast quantities of data, sacrificing privacy in the process. Also, the nontransparent, "black box" nature of conventional AI models imposes another concern of trustworthiness. Individuals and businesses remain unsure of how their data is used, processed, and who benefits from it.

Blockchain, with its decentralized, transparent, and hard-to-tamper qualities can counteract these issues, fostering a safer terrain for AI deployment by augmenting data privacy and security in unprecedented ways.

6.2. The Blockchain Revolution: Setting the Ground

The emergence of blockchain technology has been nothing short of a revolution, particularly in terms of ensuring the security and privacy of data. Its inherent characteristics: decentralization, transparency, and immutability make it a potential antidote to many of the data-related concerns today.

Blockchain's decentralization adds an extra layer of security to data. Unlike centralized systems that pose single points of failure, a decentralized blockchain distributes data across a network of peers. This distribution eliminates the vulnerability to hacking, making it extremely difficult for unauthorized individuals to compromise the system or manipulate data.

Transparency is another foundational pillar of blockchain. Each transaction on the network is visible to every participant, enhancing the system's openness. Transparency can lead to higher accountability, reducing fraudulent activities or misuse of data.

Immutability - the inability of past records to be altered - gives blockchain its trustworthiness. Once data is entered into a block in the chain, it is nearly impossible to tamper with it. This feature ensures the authenticity and reliability of data, which is critical in fields where data integrity is paramount.

6.3. Blockchain and AI Integration: A Stronghold for Data Security

Merging AI and blockchain can create a synergistic effect,

capitalizing on the strengths of each technology while mitigating their individual weaknesses. AI's cognitive capabilities combined with blockchain's security measures carve a promising path towards data privacy and security.

Firstly, a blockchain-powered AI could enforce the concept of data ownership. Data creators could decide how their data is used and by whom, owing to the granular control enabled by the blockchain technology. This increased autonomy and visibility might mitigate the uncertainty and concerns linked to data privacy.

Moreover, blockchain plays an instrumental role in ensuring the AI models' transparency. A blockchain-based record of data inputs and algorithmic operations could provide an audit trail. This traceability could allow stakeholders to understand and trust AI processes, minimizing the "black box" perception.

The application of smart contracts in AI is another fascinating intersection. Smart contracts are self-executing contracts stored on the blockchain, where the terms and conditions of the contract are written into the code. These could be leveraged to automate permissions and agreements regarding data usage in AI implementations, adding an extra layer of security and control.

6.4. Broader Applications: Industries Standing to Benefit

The fusion of blockchain and AI for data privacy and security has applications across multiple sectors.

In healthcare, patient data is considerably sensitive and needs rigorous protection. Blockchain can provide secure data storage, while AI can facilitate patient data analysis for personalized medical care. Further, blockchain could lend control to the patients, helping shape informed decisions on their health data.

In finance, blockchain and AI could create more secure, swift, and transparent processes. Banks could prevent fraudulent transactions, and customers could enjoy improved services, fostering greater trust in financial institutions.

In public governance, blockchain and AI could enable robust and transparent voting systems, minimizing possibilities of manipulation or false voting.

In conclusion, merging blockchain with AI brings us a step closer to resolving the existing data privacy and security conundrum - offering a glimmer of hope in an uncertain digital world. The interoperability of these two technologies could lead to a more reliable, secure, and fair digital future. However, realizing this potential also hinges on proper regulation and ethical considerations, urging a rigorous consideration of these elements in any blockchain-AI deployment.

Chapter 7. Revolutionizing Industries: Real-World Applications of Blockchain-Infused AI

Promised as the new backbone of our digital society, Blockchain and Artificial Intelligence (AI) have disrupted our notion of technological innovation. On the one hand, Blockchain excels in promoting security and transparency, while AI has accelerated decision-making processes and pattern recognition. The amalgamation of these two revolutionary technologies promises to herald new industrial transformations that could lead not only to economic prosperity but also to societal augmentation.

7.1. Deciphering the Convergence: Blockchain and AI

Understanding the integration of Blockchain and AI starts with considering their rudimentary definitions and functions individually. Essentially, Blockchain technology is a decentralized, distributed database, designed to chronicle digital transactions. Replicated across nodes in a peer-to-peer network, blockchains exhibit a high level of safety and transparency, immutability, and resistance to data modification. Meanwhile, AI is the simulation of human intelligence processed by machines, especially computer systems. These processes comprise learning, reasoning, self-correction, and most controversially, the ability to manipulate and interpret data.

Upon their convergence, these technologies address the deficiencies and augment the capabilities of one another, thereby creating an extraordinarily intricate yet robust system. With Blockchain's decentralized structure, it safeguards AI algorithms and data security, eliminating the central point of failure prone to cyber-attacks. Meanwhile, AI can optimize the efficiency and scalability of Blockchain, effectively reducing the hefty energy consumption associated with mining operations. This intersection presents a fusion of security, efficiency, and autonomy, which drastically amplifies the capacities of each technology, propelling diverse industry applications.

7.2. Changing the Terrain in Healthcare: Blockchain-Powered AI

One of the key sectors embracing the integration of Blockchain and AI is healthcare. With an increasing number of connected devices used in healthcare services, the need for secure management of medical records is more crucial than ever. Blockchain meets this requirement by storing patient information securely in an immutable and transparent chain of blocks. Coupling AI with Blockchain not only ensures reliable data management but also empowers AI algorithms to perform more effectively by providing large, secure datasets for training.

Take for instance, predictive analytics in prognosis and diagnosis. Powered by AI, predictive tools can scour through immense quantities of historical patient data, revealing hidden patterns and correlations that human practitioners might overlook. This process is further enhanced by Blockchain technology's ability to create vast, reliable patient databases, granting these AI tools the means to make accurate projections.

Moreover, drug discovery can experience significant acceleration, given the large datasets made available by Blockchains. AI's capabilities can be recruited to rapidly analyze these collections of data. This reduces the resources, time, and capital traditionally required in the discovery and testing process, thereby revolutionizing pharmaceutical industry operations.

7.3. Reshaping the Financial Sector

The fusion of Blockchain and AI technologies is equally transformative for the financial and banking sectors. Herein, AI can help automate decision-making processes, perform real-time fraud detection, and enable personalized financial services. Blockchain underpins the security foundation necessary for these services to be operated seamlessly and safely.

Take, for instance, the case of smart contracts. These self-executing contracts with the terms of agreement directly written into code lines can automate numerous processes in banking and insurance, such as loan distribution and claims handling. Coupled with AI, these smart contracts can be adjusted to individual circumstances, providing higher personalization and reducing manual error.

Blockchain's transparency and traceability features complement AI in fraud detection. Combining blockchain technology's immutable record of all transactions with AI's pattern recognition capabilities, financial institutions can effectively track, detect, and prevent fraudulent transactions in real-time, improving efficiency, and protecting customer assets.

The personalization of financial services is another aspect of finance revolutionized by the integration of these two technological powerhouses. Banks and financial institutions can employ AI to analyze blockchain data, creating tailored financial products and services. This improved customer intimacy leads to enhanced service quality, customer satisfaction, and customer loyalty.

7.4. Transforming Supply Chain Management

Blockchain and AI are also redefining how supply chain management functions. The integration of these technologies facilitates the next generation of traceability, efficiency, and transparency in the supply chain sector.

Blockchain technology's strong immutable record ensures that all transactional data across the supply chain is efficient, verifiable, and secure. AI is then able to leverage these credible data sets to predict and manage demand, optimize logistics, analyze and reduce risks, and significantly improve the efficiency of supply chain operations.

Track-and-trace technology, a groundbreaking application in supply chain management, dramatically benefits from the symbiosis of these technologies. Using a mix of Blockchain and AI, companies can track their products from the point of manufacture to the consumer's hands, often in real-time. This provides companies with an unprecedented level of transparency and accountability, fostering trust among stakeholders.

7.5. In Conclusion: A New Digital Frontier

In conclusion, the convergence of Blockchain and AI is leading a disruptive transformation across diverse industries. Sectors such as healthcare, finance, and supply chain management are witnessing a paradigm shift with the integration of these technologies. By weaving together the strengths of AI and Blockchain - the secure, decentralized, and transparent features of blockchain, and the rapid, real-time, predictive abilities of AI – we observe a promising future teeming with potential.

While the integration of Blockchain and AI brings about immense opportunities, it is not devoid of challenges. Issues like data privacy, regulatory readiness, and technical complexities need to be sufficiently addressed as this convergence evolves. Regardless, the revolutionary alliance of Blockchain and AI continues to drive a new age of digital innovation that has the potential to reshape our society fundamentally. The embrace or neglect of this revolutionary techno-duo will inevitably define the digital frontier of tomorrow.

Chapter 8. Limitations and Hurdles: What Could Potentially Hold Back This Tech Nexus

Understanding the limitations and hurdles in the convergence of Blockchain and AI involves unraveling the complex concerns related to technology, society, regulation, and ethical considerations. This chapter explores these potential barriers that could hinder the progress and wider adoption of this tech nexus.

8.1. Technological Challenges

At the forefront of the potential issues in integrating Blockchain and AI is the puzzle of technological compatibility. These technologies function differently and addressing the complications in their coalescence poses a significant technical challenge.

One principal issue is scalability. AI processes require vast computational resources and data storage capabilities. On the other hand, today's blockchain systems are inherently slow and lack the bandwidth for high-speed data processing. While each blockchain transaction is secure and transparent, the linear sequential nature of the ledger leads to slow transaction speeds, which contrast sharply with AI's need for rapid data processing.

Another core technical hurdle involves data privacy and management. AI algorithms often require massive data sets for their learning processes and these data need to be left in their raw, unencrypted form. However, this contradicts the primary feature of Blockchain technology - encryption of data to uphold the security and privacy of transactions. Striking a balance between data privacy and access for learning algorithms poses a critical challenge.

Moreover, the hybridization of AI and Blockchain can potentially magnify the existing individual problems in each technology. For example, the black-box problem in AI, which involves the opaqueness of decision-making processes of AI algorithms, could be exacerbated when coupled with blockchain's immutable records.

8.2. Regulatory Hurdles

The legal uncertainties surrounding both AI and Blockchain technologies add an extra layer of complication. As we step into a new era of technological innovation, our existing legal frameworks appear inadequate to address the novel challenges.

Blockchain's decentralized nature, global reach, and anonymity could potentially facilitate illegal activities, increasing regulatory concerns. On the other hand, AI's algorithmic decision-making processes can conflict with existing laws on data protection and algorithmic accountability.

Current regulatory frameworks vary significantly across different countries and often haven't kept pace with the rapid technological advancements. This absence of uniform regulatory guidelines may discourage investors and innovators, impeding the broader adoption of both technologies.

8.3. Ethical Concerns

The amalgamation of Blockchain and AI brings notable ethical concerns to the spotlight. AI's decision-making capabilities raise questions about accountability and transparency, while blockchain's immutable nature adds further complexity.

AI systems, often perceived as 'black boxes,' have raised

accountability concerns. How can we ensure those systems behave as intended? Who is liable if an AI-powered system makes a wrong decision? Pairing AI and Blockchain might raise even larger ethical dilemmas as the permanent and immutable nature of the blockchain can make errors by AI systems particularly costly and difficult to correct.

8.4. Societal Considerations

Adopting AI and blockchain technologies has important societal implications as well. There is a prevailing concern on jobs displacement due to increased automation and improved efficiency resulting from the combination of these technologies. Moreover, the societal impact of AI and blockchain on issues like privacy, equity, and access cannot be underestimated.

Moreover, the knowledge gap and the lack of public understanding of these technologies can be a significant barrier to their mass adoption. Accessibility and inclusivity issues may arise if these technologies continue to remain in the hands of a few, leading to societal disparities.

8.5. Overcoming the Hurdles: A Glance into the Future

Despite these challenges, efforts are underway to address them, pointing us towards a promising future. Technological innovations like sharding, off-chain computation, and state channels, are contemplated to solve blockchain scalability issues. Active research is ongoing to ensure privacy in AI without compromising data access for machine learning.

On the legal front, there is a push from academics and advocates for policymakers to understand these disruptive technologies better and to develop effective and inclusive regulations.

As we stand at the threshold of a new digital age with AI and blockchain at its core, understanding and addressing these limitations and hurdles is crucial. Their convergence promises a revolutionary overhaul of our systems and practices, making strides towards overcoming these challenges all the more important and urgent.

Chapter 9. Overcoming Barriers: Strides Towards Alleviating the Hurdles

Blockchain and Artificial Intelligence (AI) - two tech giants of the modern age, each with a bag full of opportunities yet hindered by substantial barriers which frequently stall their full potential realization. By addressing these challenges in unison, a combined Blockchain-AI platform can pave the way for remarkable advancements.

9.1. Understanding Barriers

The path towards completely integrating blockchain and AI in our daily lives is laden with obstacles. For AI, issues such as data privacy, model interpretability or lack of transparency, and data monopolization come to the fore. Blockchain hurdles dwell mainly in the realms of scalability, energy consumption, user-friendly interfaces and regulatory uncertainty.

AI typically thrives on large volumes of data, which often includes sensitive information. Processing and storing this data often portends potential privacy breaches. With GDPR and similar regulations in place, protecting user data is paramount. On the other hand, AI currently lacks transparency. 'Black box' models make it challenging for outsiders to understand the decision-making process, creating trust issues.

Data monopoly, another significant concern, arises when large companies monopolize the AI industry by controlling vast data streams. Regarding Blockchain, it is still striving for widespread adoption due to its technical complexity. Lack of user-friendly interfaces, poor scalability, slow transactions, and high energy consumption are problems plaguing blockchain applications presently. Additionally, uncertain regulatory stances sporadically put forth by jurisdictions worldwide hurt investor confidence and industry development.

In the subsequent sections, we will explore how these technologies can aid one another in overcoming these hurdles, and what solutions are currently in place or under development.

9.2. Fusion of AI and Blockchain

At its core, the union of blockchain and AI is about leveraging their strengths to overcome individual weaknesses. Blockchain's transparency, security, and decentralized nature can attend to AI's interpretability and privacy concerns. Similarly, AI's scalability and efficiency can help navigate the issues of energy consumption and throughput hindering blockchain implementations.

A blockchain-powered AI system establishes trust as interactions and decisions are recorded on an immutable ledger, clearing the 'black box' concern associated with traditional AI systems. Simultaneously, commingling blockchain with AI can provide a more equitable data sharing economy, thereby mitigating the monopolization issue.

AI can assist in optimizing blockchain functions; for instance, machine learning algorithms can help predict optimal energy consumption times, help reduce wastage, and improve the scalability of transactions. AI can also make blockchain more accessible by providing user-friendly interfaces.

9.3. Blockchain for AI: Current Implementations

Companies such as SingularityNET and Ocean Protocol have already begun exploiting the benefits of the fusion of AI and blockchain.

SingularityNET is developing a decentralized marketplace for AI, addressing the monopolization issue. Additionally, their system logs all AI interactions on the blockchain, making the entire process transparent and auditable.

The Ocean Protocol uses blockchain technology to create a decentralized data marketplace, enabling secure, privacy-preserving data sharing. This procedure not only exploits blockchain's data protection capabilities but also counters data monopolization by giving control back to the user.

9.4. AI for Blockchain: Current Implementations

On the flip side, AI is being employed to spruce up blockchain performance. For instance, Matrix AI Network uses AI algorithms for flexible blockchain management, meaning it can self-optimize based on the load. Additionally, AI algorithms help minimize wastage by determining optimal times for energy usage, which can lead to significant cost savings and environmental benefits.

9.5. The Road Ahead

While the fusion of blockchain and AI shows great promise, numerous challenges yet need to be addressed to fully exploit the potential of these technologies. Issues such as establishing regulatory frameworks, education and dissemination of knowledge, provision for interoperability between different systems, and more comprehensive and efficient models for energy consumption optimization are some of the territories awaiting conquest.

Meanwhile, research is in progress to fully leverage the potentials that each technology brings, and to ease the amalgamation. The convergence of the blockchain and AI continues to be among the most exciting frontiers of both technological and socio-economic transformations.

This journey towards overcoming the barriers is indeed not a sprint but a marathon, requiring ongoing effort, commitment, and constant innovation. The eventual rewards of this painstaking journey, however, promise unprecedented transformation across industries, economies, and societies. It's an insightful exploration into what could act as the pillars supporting the digital civilization of tomorrow. Consequently, all eyes remain on the technological horizon to witness how these symbiotic advancements unfold to define our collective future beautifully.

Chapter 10. Emerging Trends and Predictions: A Look into the Future of Blockchain-Powered AI

As Blockchain and Artificial Intelligence (AI) continue to evolve, their synergistic potential is apparent in various sectors. This chapter envisions the compelling future being created at the intersection of these two transformative technologies.

The narrative unfolds by first inspecting the major trends we currently observe, followed by extrapolation into probable future scenarios shaped by the confluence of Blockchain and AI.

10.1. Major Trends

Blockchain and AI have already begun to shape our digital landscape individually, demonstrating the capability to transform industries ranging from finance to healthcare. With a holistic lens, we can identify three central trends currently driving the convergence of Blockchain and AI.

1. **Data privacy revolution.** The rise of regulations like the General Data Protection Regulation (GDPR) in Europe signifies a global shift towards safeguarding user data. AI depends on data, but Blockchain can enable privacy-preserving, decentralized data storage and processing, forming a basis for developing GDPR-compliant AI applications.

2. **Decentralization of AI.** Centralized AI development has risks such as data manipulation and biased algorithms. Blockchain can instigate a shift towards decentralized AI, promoting

transparency and giving individuals control over their own data, resulting in a more equitable AI ecosystem.

3. **Interoperability across platforms.** Blockchain provides a mechanism for disparate systems to interact seamlessly, which can facilitate interactions between different AI systems, creating an interconnected network of AI models capable of learning from each other.

10.2. Predictions: A Practical Look Forward

Translating these trends into the future, yielded by this techno-duo, offers startling possibilities. Here are some informed predictions:

1. **Self-aware decentralized AI networks.** We could witness the dawn of autonomous, self-adjusting machine learning models, powered by smart contracts, capable of making independent decisions while maintaining data privacy and security.

2. **AI-driven Blockchain 'mining.'** AI could optimize proof-of-work, proof-of-stake, proof-of-location and other consensus mechanisms in Blockchain technology. AI models employing predictive analysis and optimization could deliver faster transaction processing and efficient 'mining' operations.

3. **Blockchain-powered AI marketplaces.** Imagine a decentralized marketplace for AI models, where developers can share their models in a secured, transparent platform in exchange for tokens or cryptocurrency.

4. **AI for Blockchain governance.** AI could provide a solution for one of the most heated debates in Blockchain, its governance issues. Machine learning algorithms could analyze previous decisions and network activities to propose optimized, dynamic consensus mechanisms.

5. **AI-enhanced smart contracts.** AI models can enhance the

functionality of smart contracts. Such contracts can become self-learning and adaptive over time, improving contract execution and dispute resolution.

10.3. The Promise of a Blockchain-Powered AI Future

The power of the Blockchain and AI convergence is fascinating, promising immense innovation and redefining the digital landscape. It can empower individuals, enhancing data privacy and security while driving data democratization.

In this evolving techno-duo, we can look forward to a new digital age where human-centricity, transparency, and efficiency are paramount. It unlocks new dimensions to digital transformation, beyond centralized digital commerce, opening doors to decentralized innovations in industries like healthcare, finance, supply chain management, and more.

While the decentralization of AI through Blockchain can bring a new operational lens to the digital universe, the path isn't without challenges. There remain issues around data privacy, AI interpretability, and Blockchain scalability to be tackled. Also, a balanced governance system that accommodates dynamic changes is a work in progress.

Yet, witnessing the trends and understanding the potential, it's clear that the convergence of Blockchain and AI carries transformative power. Indeed, there's no hyperbole in stating that their potent synergy promises to redefine the future of the digital world. Whether you're a digital enthusiast, entrepreneur, researcher, or simply a fascinated observer, keep your eyes on this space. It's a techno-journey worth following, promising to deliver a future where technology truly serves humanity.

Chapter 11. Conclusion: Harnessing the Power of Blockchain and AI - The Road Ahead

As we journey towards the end of this intriguing narrative, the extraordinary promise and potential of the fusion of Blockchain and AI becomes increasingly vivid. This disruptive combination, arched on the strong foundational pillars of decentralization, security, autonomy, and intelligence, is primed to usher pivotal transformations across industries, economies, and societies alike. Let's comprehend this envisioned future deeper, as we ponder over the specifics of this compelling tech duo and their transformative capabilities.

11.1. The Redevelopment of AI through Blockchain

Blockchain, with its inherent virtues of transparency and security, arms AI with an enriched toolkit to tackle one of its core challenges: trust. The enigma that engulfs the decision-making processes within AI systems often leads to a barrier in its widespread acceptance. Blockchain, by enabling traceability and verifiability, demystifies the 'black box' of AI algorithms, illuminating the path it treads to reach a certain decision. This newfound clarity is pivotal in fostering trust among users, accelerating AI's permeation across diverse applications.

Moreover, blockchain forms the bedrock for creating decentralized marketplaces for sharing AI models and datasets, incentivizing stakeholders involved and nurturing an ecosystem of symbiotic growth. The democratized access facilitates the diffusion of AI's benefits widely, unlocking previously unexplored potential.

11.2. Unleashing AI's Potential in Blockchain

On the other side of the spectrum, AI supercharges blockchain systems through its abilities in prediction, optimization, and automation. AI-based predictive analytics can intelligently anticipate potential network anomalies or breaches in blockchain infrastructures, bolstering security. Additionally, AI mechanisms can optimize complex processes such as transaction verification or mining, providing efficiency gains.

Artificial Neural Networks, a subset of AI, is particularly effective in tackling a stumbling block of blockchain scalability. These networks can reduce the necessity of storing every transaction on each node, making the blockchain structure manageable, fast, and scalable.

11.3. Sectoral Impact: A Deep Dive

Decoding the multifaceted relationship between blockchain and AI reveals their transformative potential in various sectors. It is intriguing to envision how AI-backed smart contracts can reform legal systems, or how the duo can bring about democratization in data-intensive domains like healthcare and education.

For instance, in healthcare, the data immutability characteristic of blockchain subsided with AI's predictive capabilities can revolutionize patient treatment methods, possibly saving millions of lives. Similarly, blockchain's transparent yet secure attributes amalgamated with AI's intelligent tutoring can redefine e-learning systems, making quality education accessible for all.

Not neglecting the fact that the integration of AI and blockchain into business processes makes them more streamlined and profit-oriented. This techno-duo, in essence, brings automation, security, and intelligence into business workflows, amplifying efficiency, and enhancing customer satisfaction.

11.4. Future Trends: Blockchain and AI

The intersection of AI with blockchain is not a static point but an evolving trajectory that would need continuous tracking. Increases in decentralization and privacy are crucial trends to watch.

Decentralized AI-powered blockchain systems could lead us towards a future of "decentralized intelligence," a reality where more control and power are handed back to the users. AI models could evolve to be personal AI models, protecting users' privacy while providing the bespoke assistance they require.

Another ascending trend could be the growing emphasis on "Edge Intelligence," where decision-making processes of AI are pushed to the edge of the network, facilitating real-time informed decisions. Blockchain could corroborate this with its decentralized nature, opening up the possibility of distributed AI, making intelligent systems more accessible and affordable.

11.5. Wrapping Up the Journey

To conclude, the convergence of blockchain and AI promises a future that is secure, efficient, decentralized, and smart. It's a powerful fusion that embeds trust into the fabric of complex systems interacted with on a daily basis. As we delve into this fascinating future, one thing is certain, continued exploration, understanding, and refinement of these technologies will be crucial.

The road forward also demands clear, well-placed regulations that guide without stifling innovation, and a deliberate fostering of the pool of digital talent. With these elements in place, we could witness the transformative power of AI-powered blockchain systems reaching their fullest potential, reshaping established socio-economic structures, and unveiling a new era of technological marvels.

The interweaving of Blockchain and AI is no longer a hypothetical concept but a tangible reality around us. Does it promise a garden of technological Eden or exude the aura of Pandora's Box - only the stretching canvas of time can elaborate. But despite the scepticism and projected challenges, one thing remains unequivocal - the fusion of Blockchain and AI is poised to disrupt the status quo, chalking out the outlines of a future that is unimaginable in today's terms. Let's step into this novel realm, together, with an eye on the possibilities and a heart brimming with courage. Buckle up, for we are just getting started!

www.ingramcontent.com/pod-product-compliance
Lightning Source LLC
Chambersburg PA
CBHW071012260726

48661CB00007B/2923